# FLAME IN CHALICE

**Portrait of Nicholas Roerich** by Svetoslav Roerich

# FLAME IN CHALICE

## NICHOLAS ROERICH

*Translated by* MARY SIEGRIST

NICHOLAS ROERICH MUSEUM
NEW YORK          MMXVII

Nicholas Roerich Museum
319 West 107th Street
New York NY 10025
www.roerich.org

© 1929 by Roerich Museum Press.
© 2017 by Nicholas Roerich Museum.
First edition published in 1930. Second edition 2017.

Cover illustration: Nicholas Roerich. *The Command*. 1917.

# FOREWORD TO THE FIRST EDITION

THE title of these poems—Flame in Chalice—is significant. To the discerning reader their full esoteric quality need hardly be pointed out. And even a child will be aware of the singing, flame-dipped words.

Not strangely, Nicholas Roerich is master of the singing word no less than of the singing form and color. (To the ocean-tides of the spirit, the arts are one.) His poetry is direct, simple, arrow-like. It has the same vibrant touch of the master, the same sense of mysticism and cosmic unfoldment found in his paintings. The depth and intensity, the rhythmic sweep and exaltation that mark his work as artist is no less present here. His lyric words, like so many singing arrows, fly straight to their invisible goal. Light rays out powerfully from the lines. It is evident that they have been "made in flame as nature makes."

In this brief space let us deal with the substance of the poetry of Roerich rather than with elements of form and technique, however much might be said of the unobtrusive art by means of which each word, each phrase, weaves into a victorious rhythm—part of a winged Alaya. Here, first of all, is the naturalness—the simplicity—of all art that has permanence. Here is the "wisdom of joy." Here is the rainbow quality that we find in his paintings—the promise of the future, the prophecy of dawn, of the greatness and fullness of Tomorrow.

Roerich differs strikingly from many of our acid, disillusioned so-called "moderns" in this note of belief and expectancy. "I summon the heart, wisdom and labor," he declares. And "The great Today will be dimmed Tomorrow." Life for him does not grow less but greater with the years. It is not a diminishing scale but a crescendo. This perfect spiritual world that we contact in rare moments is here, he tells us, for our discovery and inhabiting. He is the Great Believer. There *is* a quest. There *is* a pilgrimage. Therefore he is the unweariable pilgrim. Throughout the body of his poetry, one feels this spiritual awareness and prophecy, this consciousness of the sacred pilgrimage that must be made sooner or later by every human being born into the worlds. There is a Holy Grail to be found by each spiritual pilgrim. At the call of the Messenger, he must arise and gird himself for the journey. The Last Gates are stormed and entered. Often, significantly, the pilgrim journeys alone.

In the English rendering, I have tried to keep, as nearly as might be—a certain loss is inevitable—the rhythm and beat of the original lines. This was made possible only through the assistance of Miss Esther J. Lichtmann, of the Roerich Museum, who first translated the lines from the Russian, giving me their English equivalent. To her I offer my thanks and grateful appreciation.

In the poetry of Roerich, finally, there is a fullness and expansion of consciousness, a vibration of light and color, a sense of prophecy and ongoing, of search, discovery and fulfilment that is as much part of his singing word as of the colors and contours of his brush. These poems are true children of the Flame in Chalice.

MARY SIEGRIST<br>New York, August, 1929.

# CONTENTS

## Part I—Sacred Signs

| | |
|---|---|
| INVOCATION | 13 |
| SACRED SIGNS | 16 |
| WE SHALL SEE | 18 |
| AT THE LAST GATES | 20 |
| THE BEGGAR | 22 |
| TRAILS | 24 |
| CAN I BELIEVE THEM? | 25 |
| TOMORROW | 27 |
| TIME | 29 |
| INTO THE CROWD | 30 |
| IN VAIN | 31 |
| IN THE DANCE | 32 |
| I SHALL ASCEND | 33 |
| THOU SHALT SEE | 34 |
| THE GUARD | 36 |
| THE KEY FROM THE GATES | 37 |
| TO HIM | 39 |
| OUR PATH | 40 |
| I SHALL NOT REVEAL | 41 |

## Part II—To The Blessed One

| | |
|---|---|
| DROPS | 45 |
| THE HOUR | 46 |
| THE CALLING ONE | 48 |
| IN THE MORNING | 49 |

| | |
|---|---|
| BENEVOLENCE | 50 |
| REVEAL! | 51 |
| I LEFT | 52 |
| LIGHT | 53 |
| HOW SHALL I STRIVE? | 54 |
| THY SMILE | 56 |
| THEY DID NOT UNDERSTAND | 57 |
| I SHALL GUARD | 58 |
| TO THEE | 59 |
| BOTTOMLESS | 60 |
| LOVE | 62 |
| THOU HAST NOT GONE AWAY | 63 |
| "I SEE AROUND ME" | 64 |
| BY THE RULER | 65 |
| TO US | 66 |
| REJOICE | 67 |
| WITH A SMILE? | 68 |

## Part III—To The Boy

| | |
|---|---|
| THE ETERNAL | 71 |
| LIGHT | 72 |
| THE SCEPTER | 73 |
| THOU ART SENT | 74 |
| ADORN | 75 |
| INTO THE EARTH | 76 |
| WE CANNOT | 77 |
| NOT TO KILL? | 78 |
| DO NOT COUNT | 79 |
| DO NOT CLOSE | 80 |
| UNDER THE EARTH | 81 |
| THEN | 82 |
| IT WILL HELP | 83 |

| | |
|---|---|
| THE GREAT ONE WILL AVAIL | 84 |
| IN THE FACE OF ALL | 85 |
| OF THE ETERNAL | 86 |
| THOU REPEATEST | 87 |
| CHILDREN'S CASTLES | 88 |
| THEY SHALL NOT KILL | 89 |
| AT HAND | 90 |
| THOU WILT DESIRE | 91 |
| THE ACHIEVEMENT | 92 |
| LAKSHMI, THE VICTORIOUS | 93 |

## Part IV—To The Hunter Entering The Forest

| | |
|---|---|
| TO THE HUNTER ENTERING THE FOREST | 101 |

# PART I
## SACRED SIGNS

# INVOCATION

## I

Flame in chalice!
Father—fire. Son—fire. Spirit—fire.
Three equal. Three indivisible
Flame and heat—are their heart.
The fire—their eyes.
The whirlwind and the flame—their mouth.
Flame of divinity—fire.
The fire will sear the daring ones.
The flame will burn the daring ones.
The flame will stay the daring ones,
Will purify the daring ones.
Bend back the arrows of the demons.
Let the poison of the serpent descend upon
    the daring ones!
Aglamide, Commander of the Serpent,
Artan, Arion, give ear!
Tiger, eagle, lion of the desert wastes,
Guard from the evil ones!
Curl as serpent; be burned by
Fire;
Disperse, perish, O daring one!
    Flame in chalice!

## II

Father—the peaceful. Son—the peaceful.
    Spirit—the peaceful.
The three equal. The three indivisible.
The blue sea—is their heart.
The stars—their eyes.
The night dawn—their mouth.
The depth of divinity—the sea.
The daring ones walk upon the sea.
Blind to them are the arrows of the demons.
Lynx, wolf, gerfalcon,
Guard the daring ones!
Keios, Keyosavi, let them in,
    The daring ones.

## III

Know the Stone! Guard the Stone!
Hide the Flame! Be lit by fire!
By the red, the courageous;
By the blue, the peace-filled;
By the green, the wise.
Know alone. Guard the Stone!
Foo, Lo, Ho, carry the Stone.
Reward the strong.
Compensate the faithful.
Yenno-Guyo-Dja,
    Go boldly!

1911

## SACRED SIGNS

We do not know. But they know.
The stones know. Even trees
Know.
And they remember.
They remember who named the mountains
And rivers,
Who constructed the former
Cities.
Who gave the names
To the immemorial countries—
Words unknown to us—
They are filled with meaning!
Everything is filled with achievements.
Everywhere
Heroes passed. "To know" —
Is a sweet word. "To remember" —
Is a terrible word. To know and
To remember, to remember and to know
Means—to have faith.

Airships were flying.
Came pouring a liquid fire. Came flashing
The spark of life and death.
By the might of spirit stony masses
Ascended.
A wondrous blade was forged.
Scriptures guarded wise secrets.
And again all is revealed.
All new.
Fairy tale—legend—
Have become life. And we live again.
And again we shall change.

And again
We shall touch the earth.
The great "Today" shall be dimmed
Tomorrow.
But Sacred Signs
Will appear. Then
When needed.
They will be unperceived. Who knows?
But they will create
Life. And where are
    The Sacred Signs?

                                1915

## WE SHALL SEE

We go to search for Sacred
Signs. We go carefully and
In silence.
People pass by. They laugh.
They summon us to follow. Others hurry on
In discontent. Others threaten us.
They want to seize what we possess.
The passers-by
Do not know that we have gone
To search for sacred signs. But
The threatening ones shall pass.
They have so much to do. But we
Shall search for Sacred Signs.

Nobody knows where
The Host has left His signs.
Very likely they are on the milestones
Beside the road.
Or in the flowers.
Or in the waves of the river.
We think that one can quest for them
In the cloudy vaults,
By the light of the sun, by the light of the
Moon. By the light of resin
And bonfire shall we search
    For Sacred Signs.

We walk
A long time. Keenly we look.
Many people pass us by.
Verily, it seems to us, they
Know the command: to find

The Sacred Signs. Darkness falls.
It is difficult to discern
The way. Indistinguishable the paths.
Where can they be—
The Sacred Signs?.. Today, it may be
We shall not find them.
But tomorrow will be
Light. I know
    We shall
    See them.

1915

## AT THE LAST GATES

We were told "Forbidden!"
Yet we entered none the less.
We approached the gates.
Everywhere we heard "Forbidden!"
We wanted to see the signs.
We were told: "Forbidden!"
We wanted to kindle the light.
We were told: "Forbidden!"

Gray, seeing, knowing guards,
You are erring guards.
The Host has permitted to know,
The Host has permitted to see.
We guess it is His wish
That we shall know, that we shall see.

Behind the gates a messenger stands.
He brings us something.
"Let us in, guards!"
"Forbidden!" we were told.
And the gates were closed.

But none the less many were the gates
We passed. We broke our way through
And "Permitted" remained behind us.
The guards at the gates halted us.
And they begged.
And threatened.
And we were warned: "Forbidden!"
We pervaded everywhere. "Forbidden!"
All forbidden. Forbidden all.
To all forbidden.

And only behind us "Permitted."
But on the Last Gates
It will be traced "Permitted!"
And behind us "Forbidden."
Thus He commanded to inscribe
    Upon the Last Gates.

1916

## THE BEGGAR

At midnight arrived our King.
He passed to the chamber, they said.
In the morning the King came into the crowd
And we were not even aware.
We missed the sight of him.
We had to find out the commands.
But no matter; in the crowd we shall approach
And touching Him we shall say and ask:
How vast the throng! How innumerable the streets!
How many roads and trails! Lo, He could journey far.
And will He return again to the chamber?

Everywhere are footprints in the sand.
Nevertheless we shall distinguish the footprints.
A child went by. Here, a woman with a burden.
Here, no doubt, a limping one. He prostrated himself.
Is it possible we shall fail to distinguish?
Always the king has a staff.
We shall distinguish the footprints of the leaning ones.
Here, a sharp warrior point.
It does not resemble! Wider is the staff of the King
And the bearing calmer.
Well-aimed will be the taps of the staff.
Whence came so many people?
As though arranged by common consent to cross our
    path.
But we shall hasten.
I see a majestic gait, accompanied by
A peaceful and measured staff.
This perhaps
Is our King. We shall overtake and ask.

We jostled and preceded people.
We hastened.
But with the staff majestically walked
    A blind beggar.

                        1916

# TRAILS

We shall reach the King in the forest—
People shall not prevent.
There we shall ask Him.
But always the King walks alone
And the forest is overflowing with trails.
It is not known who walked this way...
The denizens of night passed by.
Silently they glided and went on their way.
By day, deserted is the forest.
Silent, the birds. Silent, the wind.
Far has gone our King.
Muted are trails and
    The ways.

## CAN I BELIEVE THEM?

Finally we learned
Whereto the King went:
To the old square of the three towers.
There He will teach.
There He will give His commands.
He will speak once. Twice
Has never spoken the King.

We shall rush to the square through an alley,
Avoiding the hurrying crowds.
We shall reach the base of the
Wind-tower. To many this path
Is unknown.
Everywhere are people.
All by-paths are crowded.
Around the passage-gates people are thronging
And there already He speaks.

Farther we shall not go.
The one who came first
Nobody knows.
But dimly is glimpsed the tower.
Sometimes it seems as though the Kingly Word
Resounds. But no.
One cannot hear the words of the King.
People are transmitting them
To each other.
A woman—to a warrior.
A warrior—to a great lord.
A shoemaker, my neighbor—
To me.
Does he

Hear them correctly from the merchant
Standing on the stoop of the porch?
    Can I believe
        Them?

## TOMORROW

I knew so many useful things
And now I have forgotten them all.
Like a robbed traveler.
Like a beggar who has lost his possessions.
In vain I remember the riches
That long since were mine;
I remember unexpectedly, not thinking,
Not knowing when the perished knowledge
Will flash.


Only yesterday I knew much
But during the night everything dimmed.
It is true the day was great.
The night was long and dark.
Came the fragrant morning.
It was fresh and wondrous
And illumined by the new sun.
I forgot and was deprived of that
Which I had gathered.
Under the rays of the new sun
All the knowledge melted.
No longer can I distinguish
An enemy from friends.
I do not know when danger
Threatens. I do not know when
Night will come. And the new sun
I shall not be able to face.
All that I once possessed,
But now I am orphaned.

Pity it is that I shall again regain
The needed not earlier than tomorrow.
But today's day is still long.
When will it come—
    The tomorrow?

## TIME

It is dreary for us to walk in the crowd.
So many hostile powers and desires.
Dark creatures descended
On the shoulders and faces of passersby.
We shall go aside; there
On the hill where the pillar stands—
An ancient one—we shall sit down.
They will pass us by.
All creatures will settle below
And we shall wait.

And if the message
About the Sacred Signs shall appear,
We too shall strive.
If they are borne aloft
We shall rise
And honor them.
Sharply we shall look,
Sharply we shall listen;
We shall be valiant and aspire
And we shall manifest—then when
Shall come the predestined
    Time.

## INTO THE CROWD

My garment is ready. Now
I shall put on the mask.
Do not wonder, my friend, if the mask
Shall terrify. This is only
A visor. We shall have
To leave our house. Whom
Shall we meet? We know not. What
Shall we see? Against the assailants
Defend ourselves with the shield.

The mask is disturbing to thee?
It does not resemble me?
Under the brow is not seen
The glance of the eye? Deeply furrowed,
    the forehead?
But soon we shall take off
The visor. And shall smile to each
Other. Now we shall enter
    The crowd.

                                      1918

## IN VAIN

Unseen are the Sacred Signs.
Let rest thine eyes.
They are tired, I know.
Close Them. I shall look for thee. I shall tell
About what I see. Hearken!
Encircling is the same plain.
The gray bushes are rustling.
The lakes sparkle like steel.
Unresponsive, the stones stand dumb.
Cold in the meadows they glisten and
Shimmer. Cold are the clouds.
They fold themselves in a furrow. They pass
Into the endless. They know, they are silent,
And guard. I see no bird.
The deer does not run on the plain.
As before, there is no one.
Nobody comes. Not one
Sign. Not one traveler.
I do not understand. I do not see. I do not know.
Thine eye thou wouldst strain
    In vain.

                                  1918

## IN THE DANCE

Fear, when the silence comes
In motion. When the strewn winds
Turn into storm. When people's speech
Shall cumber with senseless words.
Be terrified, when in the ground as treasure trove
People bury their riches.
Fear, when they consider
Safe the treasures only
On their bodies. Fear, when at hand
Crowds gather. When they forget
About knowledge. And with joy will destroy
What was learned before. And with ease execute
Threats. When there shall not be
Whereon to inscribe one's knowledge. When the leaves
Of writing become unsteady,
And the words mischievous, O my neighbors!
You builded darkly for yourselves. You overturned
Everything. There is no mystery farther than the
Present. And with the sacks of unhappiness
You went wandering and to conquer
The world. Your madness has called the most
Hideous woman, "Desired one!"
You are ready to drown yourselves
    In the dance.

1916

## I SHALL ASCEND

Once more shall my voice resound.
Whither did you go from me?
Your voices deafened
On the rocks. No more can I distinguish
Your voice from
A falling branch—from the flight
Of a migrating bird. My calls
To you also were drowned.
I do not know whether you will go
But I still long
To reach the height. The stones
Already stand bare. The moss becomes
Fainter, and the juniper
Withers and stands weakly.
Your rope would be useful
To me too; but also alone
    I shall ascend.

1917

## THOU SHALT SEE

"What warms my face?"

"The sun shines. It fills
With warmth our garden."

"What resounds?"

"The sea resounds. Although behind
The rocky mountain, it is unseen."

"Whence the fragrance of almond trees?"

"The bird-cherry tree is blossoming.
White blossoms overflood
The trees. Apple trees are also
In blossom. Multi-colored,
Everything glimmers."

"What lies ahead?"

"Thou standest on the hill.
Before us a garden slants.
Behind the meadow, the bay rises blue.
On the other side are hills and
Forests. The pine mountains are
Darkening. The outlines are lost
In the blue space."

"When shall I
See all that?"

"Tomorrow
    Thou shalt see."

                              1917

## THE GUARD

"Guard, tell me why
Thou dost close this door? What
So constantly dost thou guard?"

"I guard
The secret of this chamber."

"But empty is the
Chamber. Worthy people
Have declared: 'There is nothing in it.'"

"The secret of the chamber I know.
To guard it, I am appointed."

"But empty is thy chamber!"

"For thee it is empty!" answered the guard.

## THE KEY FROM THE GATES

"An enchanter I shall be today
And failure transmute to success."

The silent ones began to dispute.
Those about to leave turned back.
The hostile began to waver.
The threatening ones drooped.
Thoughts that came like a dove
Were received for the governance of the world.
The most peaceful words brought
A tempest. And thou walkedst like a shadow of that
Which had to happen.
And thou shalt become a child
In order that shame shall not hinder thee.

Thou wast sitting at the gates of the passers-by
Accessible to every rogue.
Thou askedst who wanted to defraud
Thee? ... Is it astonishing? ...
A successful hunter shall find
A worthy hunt. He shall find it without fear.

But, achieving my quarry,
Leaving, I know that not all of you
I have seen. The best
Meetings remained without
An issue. And many worthy ones
Passed by or
Have not yet attained. But I did not know them.
And disguised I sat amidst you.

And you wrapped yourselves
In different webs. Silently
You guarded the rusty keys
    Of the gates.

                          1917

## TO HIM

Finally I found the hermit.
You know how difficult it is
To find here on earth a hermit.
I asked him whether he would show me
The path and would he accept
Graciously my works?

He gazed a long time and asked
What is the most loved that I have.

"The most beloved?" I answered.
"Beauty it is."

"The most beloved
Thou must leave."

"Who commands it?" I asked.

"God," answered the hermit.

"Let God punish me—
I shall not leave the most beautiful
That will lead us
    To Him."

1920

## OUR PATH

Travelers, now we are passing
A country road. The farms
Alternate with fields and woodlands.
Children are taking care
Of the herds. Children approach us.
A boy gives us whortleberries
In a reed-basket. A young girl extends
A handful of fragrant grasses. A little lad
Gives up to us
His serrated little cane.
He thinks with it
We shall walk more lightly.

We are passing on.
Never again shall we meet
These children.
Brothers, we went not far
From the farms
But you are already tired of gifts.
You have scattered the fragrant grasses.
You have broken the little reed basket.
You have thrown into the gutter the little cane
Given by the young lad. Why do we need
It? On our long path.
But the children had nothing else.
They have given us the best of what
They had to adorn
    Our path.

                               1917

## I SHALL NOT REVEAL

Leave thy smile, O my friend.
Thou dost not know what
I have hidden here. Without thee
I have filled this chest.
Without thee I have covered it with a web
And I have turned the key in the lock.
To probe thou shall not succeed.
And if thou wouldst gossip
Thou wouldst have to speak falsely.
Invent, falsify, to thy need.
But the treasure-chest again
    I shall not reveal.

1917

# Part II

# TO THE BLESSED ONE

## DROPS

Thy benevolence fills
My hands. In profusion it is pouring
Through my fingers. I shall not
Keep all. I am not able to distinguish
The glowing streams of richness. Thy
Benevolent wave pours through the hands
Upon earth. I do not see, who will gather
The precious fluid? The tiny sprays,
Upon whom will they fall? I shall not have time
To reach home. Out of all the benevolence,
In my tightly holding hands I shall bring only
    Drops.

                                        1920

# THE HOUR

Awaken, O friend. A message has come.
Ended, thy rest.
Now I have learned where is guarded
One of the Sacred Signs.
Think of the joy if
One sign we shall find.
Before sunrise we shall have to go.
At night we must all prepare.
Look at the night-sky.
It is beautiful as never before;
I do not remember
Such another.
Only yesterday
Cassiopeia was sad and misty,
Aldebaran twinkled fearfully
And Venus did not appear.
And now they are all ablaze.
Orion and Arcturus are shining.
Far behind Altair
New starry signs
Are gleaming and the mistiness
Of the constellations is clear and transparent.

Dost thou not see The path to that
Which tomorrow we shall find?
The starry masses have awakened.
Take thy fortune.
The armor we shall not need.
The shoes put tightly on,
Tightly girdle thyself,

Our path will be stony.
The East is aflame.
For us
    Is the hour.

                                          1916

## THE CALLING ONE

Thou, Coming One, in the night-silence,
They say Thou art unseen,
But this is not true.
I know hundreds of people
And each has seen Thee
    at least once.
A few poor and ignorant ones
Did not succeed in seeing Thine image.

Thou changing, many-guised!
Thou dost not want to hinder our
Life. Thou dost not want to terrify us.
And Thou passest by in silence and in stillness.
Thine eyes can sparkle,
Thy voice can thunder,
And the hand can be heavy
Even for black stone.
But Thou dost not sparkle,
Thou dost not thunder,
Thou dost not bring forth destruction. Thou
    knowest
That destruction is less than rest.
Thou knowest that stillness
Is louder than thunder. Thou knowest
In the stillness, Coming and
    Calling One.

1916

## IN THE MORNING

I do not know and I cannot.
When I desire, I think—
Perhaps someone has a stronger desire?
When I know—
Does one know with knowledge still stronger?
When I can—cannot someone
Better and deeper?
And so I do not know and I cannot.

Thou, Coming One, in the stillness
Tell mutely what I have desired
In life and what attained?
Lay Thy hand on me—
I shall again desire and be valiant
And the desired of the night-hours will be known
    In the morning.

1916

## BENEVOLENCE

My gift accept, O dear friend.
Through labor and knowledge I gathered
This gift. In order to give it
I gathered it. I knew I would give it
Away. On my gift thou shalt pile
The joys of spirit. Silence and quietude.
Amidst the revolt of spirit, direct thine eye
Upon my gift.
And if thou wantest to command the servant
To bring the gift,
Name it
    Benevolence.

                                         1918

# REVEAL!

On Thy shelves along the walls
Many phials are standing.
Vari-colored they are. Carefully
All of them are closed. Some are wrapped
Tightly, that light shall not penetrate.
What is in them?—I do not know—
But austerely Thou dost guard them.
Remaining alone at night
The fires Thou lightest and a new
Creation Thou makest.
Thou knowest the purpose of creation;
Thy help I need;
In Thy creations do I believe.
The one useful
For me, that one now
    Reveal!

1917

# I LEFT

I am prepared for the road.
All that was mine I renounced.
You will take it, my friends.
Now for the last time, I shall survey
My house. Once more
I shall view my possessions. Upon the images
Of friends I shall look once more.
For the last time.
I know already
That here nothing of mine remains.
Possessions and all that impeded me
Freely I am giving away. Without them
I shall be more free. Before the One
Who calls me, liberated
I shall appear.
Now once more
I shall survey the house. View once more
That from which I am released,
Free and liberated and firm
In thought. The images of friends and the view
Of my former things
Do not confuse me. I am going. I am hurrying.
But once more—for the
Last time I shall survey all that
    I left.

1918

## LIGHT

How shall we behold Thine Image?
The all-penetrating Image,
Deeper than feeling and reason.
The intangible, the silent,
The unseen. I summon
The heart, wisdom and labor.
Who has apprehended that which has
No form, no sound, no taste,
Which has no end and no beginning?
And the darkness when all shall cease?
The thirst of the desert and the salt of the
Ocean?

I shall await Thy
Glory.
Before Thine image
The sun does not shine. The moon does not
Shine. Nor the stars nor the flame
Nor the lightning. The rainbow does not shine.
The Light of the North does not glimmer.
There shines Thine Image.
Everything gleams through Thy light.
In the darkness are shining
Particles of Thy glory.
And in my closed eyes
    Dawns Thy wondrous light.

1918

## HOW SHALL I STRIVE?

You beautiful birds of Khomas,
You do not like the earth. You
Will never descend
Upon earth. Your birdlings
Are being born in cloudy
Nests. You are nearer to the sun.

Let us think about Him, the radiant One.
But the daughters of earth are miracle-workers.
On the summits of the mountains and at the bottom
Of the sea, zealously search. Thou
Shalt find the glorious stone
Of love. In thy heart
Search for Vrindavan—the abode
Of love.
Zealously search and
Thou shalt find. Let the ray of wisdom
Penetrate us. Then
All movable shall establish itself.
The shadow shall become body.
The spirit of air shall turn into
Firm land. Sleep shall change into a
Thought. We shall not be
Carried away by tempest. Let us restrain
The winged horses of morning.
Let us direct the tides of the evening
Winds. Thy Word—is an ocean
Of truth. Who is piloting
Our boat to the shore?
Do not be afraid of Maya. Her
Immeasurable force and power we shall transcend.

Hearken! Have you ended
Discussions and quarrels? Farewell,
Aranyani! Farewell, silver
And gold of the heavens! Farewell,
Silent forest!
What song shall I dedicate to thee?
    How shall I strive?

                                  1916

## THY SMILE

At the wharf we embraced each other and said farewell.
In the golden waves the boat disappeared.
We are—on an island. Our old house.
The key of the temple—is with us. Our cave.
Ours are also the rocks and the pines and the seagulls.
Ours—the lichens. Our stars—above us.
We shall survey the island. We shall return
Home only at night. Tomorrow,
Brothers, we shall rise early.
So early, even before the sun has
Yet risen. When the East
Is lighted by a vivid radiance,
When only the earth is awake.
People will yet be sleeping.
Liberated, beyond their concerns,
We shall find ourselves. We shall be
As though we were no longer men. We shall reach the border-line
And look in. In silence and stillness.
And the Silent One will answer.
Morning, tell me what thou hast seen off
Into the darkness and what again welcomes
    Thy smile.

                                  1918

## THEY DID NOT UNDERSTAND

I do not know, when is your word strong?
Sometimes you become ordinary.
And, quietly, you sit between
The foolish ones, who know so
Little. Sometimes you speak, and it seems that
You are not upset, if you are not understood.
Sometimes you look so gently
Upon the ignorant, that I envy
Their ignorance. As if you do not care
To reveal your face. And when
You listen to the speeches of the past,
You even lower your eyes, as if
You are choosing the simplest words.
How difficult it is to discern all your
Intentions. How hard it is to
Follow you. So yesterday,
When you spoke to the bears.
It seemed to me, that they left,
    Without understanding you.

1920

## I SHALL GUARD

Come nearer to me, luminous One;
I shall not distress Thee with anything.
Yesterday Thou wantedst to approach
But my thoughts wandered and mine eyes
Roved. I could not see
Thee. When Thou hadst departed,
I felt Thy breath,
But already it was late. But today
I shall leave all that hindered me.
The thoughts I shall submerge in silence.
In the joy of spirit I shall forgive all
The malevolent ones today. Quiet
I remain. Nothing disturbs me.
Sounds of casual life
Do not distress me. I await. I know Thou wilt not
Leave me. Thou wilt
Approach me. Thine image in silence
   I shall guard.

1917

## TO THEE

What became of friendship
When I was admitted
Into the hundred-gated ashram?
If thy friend, formerly dear to Thee,
    has angered Thee,
Do not punish him, O Mighty,
According to what he deserves. All say
That thou hast forsaken us.
When With comforted heart, shall I see
Thee reconciled? Accept!
The source of my words Thou knowest.
Here are the sins and my achievements!
I am bringing them to Thee.
Take the one and the other.
Here are knowledge and ignorance!
Take the one and the other.
The devotion to Thee, leave me!
Here are purity and muddiness!
I want neither one nor the other!
Here are good and harmful thoughts.
The one and the other I bring to Thee.
Dreams leading to sin, and
Dreams of truth I offer Thee.
Grant that I may remain
With devotion and love
    To Thee.

1917

## BOTTOMLESS

Thou, Mighty, art everywhere and in all.
Thou awakenest us to the light,
Thou foldest us in sleep in the darkness,
Thou leadest us while erring.

We wanted to go blindfold, not knowing
Where. Three days we erred.
With us were fire, armor and garments.
Around us many birds and wild deer.
What more? Above us, sunsets—
Sunrises—spicy, fragrant winds.

First we traversed a large valley.
Green were the fields and the vistas so blue.
Then we traversed mossy marshes on the other side.
Juniper blossomed. From rusty
Mosses we turned aside. Depthless
Windows we avoided. Closely we followed
The sun. Clouds gathered. We hearkened
To the winds. On the moist hand we
Were catching their waves. The winds died out.
The woods thinned. We went along a rocky
Crest. Like white bones
The juniper trees stood out. Through light
Veins masses of stones impacted
In the ancient work of creation.
They climbed downward through
Crevices. Behind the crests of rocks
Was nothing seen. Night lowered.

On the steps of the giant temple
We shall descend lower. Clouds. It becomes
Dark. Below mists
Spread. The steps become steeper
And steeper. With difficulty we climb down
On the moss. Below the foot can
Touch nothing. Here we
Shall lodge overnight. On the mossy parapet
We shall slumber until morning. A long
Silent night.

Awakening, we heard
Only the whistling of dimmed flights.
In rhythmic tremor came the distant groan.
The East flushed with dawn. Mists covered
The valley. Sharp as ice
In blue masses, they impacted
Tightly. For a long time we sat outside
Of the world. Until the mists dispersed.
Above us rose a wall.
Beneath us an abyss loomed blue,
    Bottomless.

1918

## LOVE

What a day! So many people
Came to us at once.
They brought with them some
Unknown to us. Ere their coming
I could not ask about them.
Most dismaying, they spoke
In unknown languages.
And I smiled, listening to their
Strange speeches.

The tongue of some
Resembled the cry of mountain
Eagles. Others hissed like serpents.
The barking of dogs I sometimes recognized.
Like metal sparkled the speeches. The words
Became threatening. Through them
Thundered the mountain stones.
Through them poured the hail.
Through them the waterfall sang.
But I smiled. How could I
Know the meaning of their speech? They
In their own language, it may be,
Repeated the word so dear to us—
    Love.

1920

## THOU HAST NOT GONE AWAY

The work begun Thou didst leave me.
That I continue it Thou dost desire.
I feel Thy faith in me.
I shall fulfil the work attentively
And austerely. Thou hast done this work
Thyself. I shall sit at Thy
Table. I shall take Thy pen.
I shall spread Thine objects as
Before. Let them help me.
But much was not revealed by Thee
When Thou departedst. Before the windows
Of the merchants there is noise and clamor.
The footfall of horses is heavy upon
The stones. And the clangor of the iron-covered
Wheels. Beneath the roof is the whistling of
The winds. The creaking of the rigging at the
Harbor. And the heavy impact of the
Anchors. And the moaning of the
Sea-birds. I could not ask Thee:
Did this disturb Thee?
Whether from all that lives
Thou hast drawn inspiration? As far as I know,
In all the decisions from earth
    Thou hast not gone away.

                                    1919

## "I SEE AROUND ME"

A stranger made his dwelling
Near our garden. Every morning
He plays on the psaltery
And sings his song. We think
Sometimes that he repeats
The song; but the song of the unknown one
Is always new. And always people
Are crowding near his gate.

Time passed.... Now our brother
Began his work and our sister was
Betrothed. But the unknown one
Kept on singing.
We went to invite him
To sing at the sister's betrothal.
And thereupon we asked
Whence does he take the new
Words and how for such a long time
Is his song always new?

He was astonished, so it seemed, and
Straightening his white beard, said:
"It seems to me but yesterday
I took my dwelling near you. I have not yet
Had time to tell
Of all the splendor
    I see around me."

1919

## BY THE RULER

Again a messenger. Again Thy
Command! And a gift from Thee!
Ruler, Thou hast sent me
Thy pearl, and hast commanded
To include it in my string.
But Thou knowest, Ruler,
My necklace is not genuine.
And it is long—as long
As only things unreal
Can be. Thy radiant
Gift amidst the dull
Toys shall drown. But Thou
Hast commanded. I shall fulfill.

Ye street merry-makers!
On my string is a
Pearl
Bestowed on me
    By the Ruler!

1920

## TO US

In life there is so much of wonder.
Every morning near our shore
Swims by an unknown singer.
Every morning slowly from behind the mist
Moves a light boat and
A new song always rings.
And as always the singer
Is hiding behind the next crag.
And it seems to us we shall never
Know who he is—this
Singer—nor whereto he is directing his path
Every morning. And to whom
Does he sing always the new song?
Oh, what hope fills
The heart and to whom does he sing?
Maybe
    To us.

1920

## REJOICE

Behind my window the sun again
Is shining. In rainbow are clad
The little
Grass-blades. On the walls are unfolded
The brilliant banners of light. From joy
Trembles the vigilant air.
Why art thou not quiet, my spirit? Wast thou
    frightened
By that which thou dost not understand? For thee
The sun covered itself with darkness. And the dance
Of the joyous grass-blades drooped.

But yesterday thou knewest so little,
My spirit. Just as great
As thine ignorance. But from the tempest
All was so poor that thou
Hast considered thyself rich. And the sun
Shone for thee today. For thee
The banners of light unfurled.
The grass-blades brought thee joy.
Thou art rich, my spirit. To thee
Comes knowledge. The banners of light
Are shining above thee.
    Rejoice!

1918

## WITH A SMILE?

Messenger, my Messenger!
Thou standest and smilest
And thou dost not know what thou hast brought
Me. Thou hast brought me the gift
Of healing. Each tear of mine
Shall heal the wounds of the world.

But, Ruler, whence shall I
Take so many tears and to which
Of the wounds of the world shall I give
My first torrent?

Messenger,
O my Messenger, thou standest
And smilest. Dost thou not have
A command to heal sorrow
    With a smile?

1921

# Part III

# TO THE BOY

## THE ETERNAL

Boy, thou sayest
That towards evening, thou makest ready to leave
Beloved Boy, do not delay;
In the morning we shall leave with thee.

We shall enter the fragrant forest
Amidst silent trees,
In the cool glimmer of the dew.
Under light and radiant cloud
We shall take the road with thee.
If thou goest slowly, it means
Thou dost not yet know, what is
The source and joy, the primordial, and
    The eternal.

1916

## LIGHT

Boy, with a whole-hearted sorrow
Thou hast told me that the day becomes shorter,
That again the day becomes darker.

It is that a new joy may be created:
The exultation for the birth of light.
The coming joy I know.
We shall await it patiently.
But now as the day becomes shorter,
Wordlessly saddened, we say farewell
    To the light.

1916

## THE SCEPTER

All I have heard from grandfather
I repeat to thee, my boy.
From grandfather heard also my grandfather.
Every grandfather speaks;
Every grandchild listens.
To thy grandchild, my beloved boy,
Thou wilt relate all that thou learnest.

They say that the seventh grandchild will fulfill.
Do not fret overmuch if
Thou shouldst not do all as I have said.
Remember that we are still human.
But I can strengthen thee.
Break off from the nut-tree
A branch; carry it in front of thee.
It will help thee to see
Under the ground, that given by me—
    The scepter.

1915

## THOU ART SENT

Do not approach here, my child.
There, around the corner, are playing the grown-ups.
They are screaming and throwing various things;
Easily they can harm thee.
People and animals, do not touch while they play.
Fierce are the games of grown-ups.
Thy game they do not resemble.
They are not like a wooden shepherd
And submissive sheep, with pasted wool.
Stand by—they will tire,
The games of the people will end
And thou shalt go there—where
    Thou art sent.

                      1916

## ADORN

Boy, beware of things.
Often the object that we possess
Is filled with snares and malice
More dangerous than all upheavals.
With us we carry for years an evil-doer
Not knowing that this is our enemy.
At the counsel of property, a small
Knife is always hostile to us.
Hostile is also a staff.
Often a rising upheaval are
Lamps, benches and bolts.
The books disappear, we do not know where.
To the upheaval sometimes adhere
The most peaceful objects;
To save one's self from them is impossible.
Under fear of deadly revenge
You live long years,
And during the hours of reflection and boredom
You caress the enemy.
If one is spared from people
Then he is helpless against objects.

Many-colored are shining all thy things.
Thy life with benevolence
    Adorn.

1915

## INTO THE EARTH

Boy, remain calm.
The priest said a prayer above the departed one.
Said a mute prayer.
He addressed him thus:
"Thou ancient one, imperishable,
Thou everlasting, eternal, thou striving to the heights,
Joyous, reborn."

The relatives pleaded:
"Pray aloud
That we may hear.
The prayer consoles us."

"Do not disturb. I shall end,
Then I shall speak aloud
And address the body, that went
    Into the earth."

1915

## WE CANNOT

Thou thinkest thou hast finished?
Three questions answer: How can I find out
How many years a crow lives?
To the farthest star
How great is the distance?
What do I now desire?

Friend, again we do not know.
Again all is unknown to us.
Again must we begin.
    Nothing has end.

1916

## NOT TO KILL?

The boy killed a beetle.
He wanted to examine it.
The boy killed a bird
In order to study it.
The boy killed an animal
Only for knowledge.

The boy asked if he might also
For the common welfare and for knowledge
Kill a man?

"If thou hast killed a beetle, a bird and an animal,
    Why should'st thou not kill a man?"

1916

## DO NOT COUNT

Boy, give no meaning to quarrel.
Remember, the grown-ups—are strange people.
Having said about each other the most evil,
Tomorrow they are ready to call the enemies their
    friends.
And to the savior—their friend—to send an offense.

Persuade thyself to think that the mischief
Of people is shallow. Think better
Of them—but enemies and friends
    Do not count.

1916

## DO NOT CLOSE

Bending over the well
The boy exclaimed in ecstasy:
"What a beautiful sky!
How it is reflected!
It is self-colored, bottomless!"

"My beloved boy,
Thou art enchanted only by the reflection.
It is enough for thee—what is below.
Boy, do not look downward:
Upward turn thine eyes:
Know to see the great sky.
With thine own hands, thine eyes
    Do not close."

1916

## UNDER THE EARTH

Again we found skulls.
But there were no signs on them.
One was split with
An ax. The other pierced
With an arrow. But not for us
Are these signs. Crowded
They were lying, without names, all
Resembling each other. Under them
Were scattered coins
And erased were their faces.

Dear friend, thou hast guided me
Falsely. The sacred signs
Shall we not find
    Under the earth.

1907

## THEN

Thou are mistaken, boy! There is no evil.
The Great One could not create evil. There is imperfection.
But it is just as dangerous as that
Which thou callest evil.
There is no king of darkness and demons.
But with each deed
Of ignorance, falsity, anger,
We create numberless creatures,
Ugly and terrifying in their aspect,
Bloodthirsty and hideous.

They follow us,
Our creations! Their dimensions
And their aspect are created by us.
Beware of swelling their swarm.
Thine offspring will commence
To devour thee. Carefully
Touch the crowd. To live is a trial.

My boy, remember the command:
Not to fear life and to believe,
To remain free and strong
And then thou wilt attain to love.
The dark creatures do not thrive under
All this. They wither and perish
    Then.

1916

## IT WILL HELP

Boy, again thou hast erred.
Thou hast said that
Thou believest only thy feelings.
It is praiseworthy for the beginning but how
To be with emotions
That are unknown to thee now
But known to myself?
And in thy first feelings
Which thou possessest,
As thou thinkest—
Verily, thou art not yet perfect.

Hast thou mastered thy hearing?
Thy sight is still poor.
Coarse is thy touch.
Of the feelings unknown,
If thou dost not believe me,
I shall show thee a drop of water
To examine alone with thine eye.
Shall I tell thee of the
Inhabited air? Thou smilest.
Thou art silent. Thou dost not make answer.

Boy, the guidance of Spirit
Oftener invoke.
In life
    It will help.

1916

## THE GREAT ONE WILL AVAIL

Approach, boy; do not fear.
The grown-ups have taught thee to fear.
People can only frighten.
Thou hast grown without fear.
The whirlwind and the darkness, water and
    space—
Nothing has frightened thee.
The unsheathed sword exalted thee.
Towards the fire thou hast stretched thy hands.

Now thou art frightened;
Everything becomes hostile.
But do not fear me.
I have a secret Friend:
Thy fears He will dispel.
When thou fallest asleep
I shall call Him to thy bedside—
The One who is powerful.
He will whisper a word—
Courageous thou wilt rise.
    The Great One will avail.

1916

## IN THE FACE OF ALL

Thou wantest to weep and thou dost not know
Whether thou hast the right. Thou fearest to weep
Because many people gaze
At thee. Shall one shed tears
In the sight of all? But the source of thy tears
Is wonderful. Thou
Wantest to weep for the innocently
Perished. Thou wantest to shed
Tears over the young warriors
For the good. Over all who gave
All their joys for the victory
Of others—for the sorrow of others. Thou
Wantest to weep over them.

How shall it be
That others may thy tears not see?
Come nearer to me.
I shall cover thee with my garment
And then thou canst weep.
But I shall smile and all
Will believe that thou hast jested
And laughed. Maybe thou hast
Whispered me words of merriment.
Laugh one may
    In the face of all.

1916

## OF THE ETERNAL

Why didst thou want to tell me
Something unpleasant? My answer
Is ready. But first tell
Me. Think well. Declare!
Wilt thou never change
Thy belief? Wilt thou remain
Faithful to that which thou hast lanced against
　　me?

About myself, know
My answer—I am here to forget.

Look, while we spoke
Already all around us has changed.
All becomes new. That which
Threatened us, summons us now.
That which summoned us, vanished.

We ourselves have changed.
Above us the sky is transformed
And altered, the wind. The rays of the sun
Shine otherwise. Brother, let us leave
All that is fleeting. Otherwise
We shall have no time
To think of that which
For all is unchanging. To think
　　Of the eternal.

　　　　　　　　　　　　　　1917

## THOU REPEATEST

Thou art silent? Do not fear to speak.
Thou thinkest that thy tale
I know—that thou hast told it to me
Already many times?

Verily, I have heard it
From thee not once.
But caressing were thy words;
Thine eyes sparkled softly.
Thy tale repeat once more.

Every morning we enter the garden.
Every morning we rejoice before
The sun. And the spring wind
Repeats its rustling.
With the warmth of the sun wrap
Thy dear tale.
With the fragrant word,
Like the spring wind,
Smile in thy tale.
And look as radiant
As always, when thy tale
    Thou repeatest.

1918

## CHILDREN'S CASTLES

On the powerful column of a temple sits
A birdling. On the street children
Build out of mud unconquerable
Castles. How much movement flutters around
This play! The rain has washed away
Their strongholds during the night and the horse
Tramped down their towers. But
Meanwhile, let the children build
A castle out of mud and let
A birdling sit on the column.
Going towards the temple, I shall not approach
The column, but pass by
    The children's castles.

1920

## THEY SHALL NOT KILL

I have done as I desired.
Good or evil, I know not.
Do not run away from the wave, child.
If thou dost run—it will break, overturn.
But face the wave and bend
And accept it with firm soul.

I know, boy, that my hour is come
To fight. Strong is my weapon.
Stay, my boy, behind me.
Of the creeping enemy tell...
What lies ahead, is not terrifying.
No matter how they assail,
Be firm. They shall not
    Kill thee.

1916

## AT HAND

The spear we shall thrust into earth.
Ended is the first battle;
Mighty, my tempered sword;
Calm was my spirit and valiant.
But during the battle, I saw, boy,
That thou wast distracted by glamor of flowers,
When we encounter the host
Aflame be with battle, my child.
Believe in the nearness of victory.
With an eye unflinching of steel
Keenly look around thee
Whether battle is needed—
If victory dwells in thy spirit.

Let us delight in the flowers,
Rejoice in the sighs of the dove;
In the brook let us cool our faces.
Behind the rock who has hidden?
To the battle! The host
    Is at hand!

1916

## THOU WILT DESIRE

As sign of the victory, child,
Do not garb thyself
In a colorful garment.
Victory passed, but the battle will be.
They shall fail to defeat thee
But surely will come the encounter.

Thy past life perceiving
I behold glorious victories
And how many sorrowful signs!
But victory is destined for thee
If victory thou wilt
    Desire.

1917

## THE ACHIEVEMENT

Glowing with rapture
The boy brought benevolent message—
That all shall ascend the high mountain.
Exodus of the people he was commanded to tell.

A sacred message, but my dear
Little envoy, quickly
Change one word.
When thou farther hast gone
Thou wilt call thy luminous
Message, not an "exodus,"
But thou wilt say
    "The achievement"!

1916

## LAKSHMI, THE VICTORIOUS

To the east of the mountain Zent-Lhamo,
In a resplendent garden, lives the Blessed
Lakshmi, Goddess of Happiness. By unending
Toil she beautifies her seven veils of peace.
This is known to all men. All men pay
Reverence to the Goddess Lakshmi!

But all fear her sister, Siva Tandava.
She, the Goddess of Destruction, is full of
Malice, terrible and destructive.

From behind the mountains came
Siva Tandava herself. The terrible one
Went straight toward the dwelling of Lakshmi
Cautiously the terrible goddess approached
The palace of Light and lowering her voice,
Called out to Lakshmi.

Lakshmi laid aside her precious veils and
Came forth to meet her.

Lakshmi, walking, disclosed her body.
Large were her eyes, her hair was dark.
Her armlets were golden. Her many necklaces
Were of pearls. The nails of Lakshmi were of
The color of amber. Over her breasts and
Shoulders, and on her abdomen and down to
Her feet were poured unguents of special sacred
Herbs. Lakshmi and her maidens are as
Sparklingly pure as the images of
The Temple of Mathura after the storm.

But all righteousness became stricken at sight
Of the dreaded Siva Tandava, so terrifying
Was she even in her apparent humility. From out
Her canine jaw were thrust threatening fangs.
So red was her body and so shamelessly hirsute,
That it was indecent to look upon. Even the armlets
Of blood-red rubies could not beautify Siva Tandava.
One might even imagine her a man.

The Terrible one spoke:
"Hail to you, Lakshmi, righteous one, my near one!
Much happiness and welfare hast thou created.
Even too zealously didst thou perform thy work.
Thou adornest temples with gold. Thou enrichest
The earth with gardens. Thou Protectress of Beauty!

"Thou hast created the rich and the generous.
Thou hast created the poor, unreceiving yet rejoicing.
Thou hast ordained peaceful trade.
Thou hast planted among men all ties called benevolent.
Thou hast conceived of joyous frail distinctions for man
Thou hast filled the hearts of people with
The joyous realization of their superiority and pride.
Thou art generous!

"Thy maidens are tender and caressing.
Thy youths are strong and aspiring.
Joyously, people create according to their own likeness.
People forget about change and destruction.
Hail to Thee!

"Calmly you observe the human procession.
And there is little left for Thee to do!
I worry over thee, my near one!

Without labor, without worries, thy body
Will become heavy. And the precious pearls
Will fade upon it. Thy face shall shine and
Thy lovely eyes shall become bovine.

"Then will the people forget to bring pleasant
Offerings for Thee. They will bring sacred
Flowers no longer. And you will no longer
Find any excellent workers for Thyself.
All the sacred designs will become entangled.
People cannot remain inactive. Here I am,
Full worrisome about thee, Lakshmi, my near one!

"During long nights I have conceived a labor for
Thee. We are akin to each other. Do not pay
Attention to the exterior. Hard is it for me
To await the lengthy destruction of time.
Let us unite and let us annihilate all human
Structures. Let us demolish all human joys.
Let us eject all the foundations accumulated
By men. Do not be so assured that people
Follow Thee. People dimly perceive the boundaries.

"Tear down Thy seven veils of peace. And then
I shall rejoice and at once accomplish my tasks,
So that you may be aflame with zeal and creation.
And again you shall shed benevolent tears over
Men and again you may weave still more ornamental
Veils for Thyself. You shall create still richer
Ornaments. You, the inexhaustible Giver!
Again people will search for Thee.

"In humiliation once more they will accept
With gratitude Thy gifts. Thou shalt conceive
For men so many small new conditions and

Petty inventions that even the most foolish
Will think himself clever and important.
I do not fear the human curse and already
Perceive the joyous tears offered to Thee by men!

"Ponder deeply, Lakshmi, my near one!
My thoughts are useful to Thee and to me,
Thy sister, they are full of joy."

A cunning power has Siva Tandava. Only think!
She recalled the past wars and human miseries.
Only think! Again she wished to evoke upon earth
The destruction through evil. Only think!
What evil notions reawoke in this malicious brain.

But not one word did Lakshmi say in response.
Silently, only by a gesture, she rejected
The evil project of Siva Tandava.

Then once again the evil Goddess, ready with
Threats and grinding her fangs, and forgetful of
All her previous benevolent approaches began:
"Foolish Lakshmi! You surround yourself
With these peaceful female embroiderers.
They cherish the small walls of their
Miserable homes. Bent over their earthly
Designs they forget to look at the stars.
They forget the threatening conjunction of stars.
People cannot grasp that which comes in peace.
They revere the thunder and lightning.

"Thy old altars are covered with fetid grease.
Thy beauty cannot dwell in the dust of old houses.
The best designs are destroyed by time and

The best pattern is covered with mold. Follow me!
I will show Thee such chorus of conceit that
Thy wisdom shall be confounded!"

Such fearful things did Siva Tandava utter.
And earthquakes pierced the earth with
Their convulsions. And islands sank into
The oceans. And new mountains rose.
But Lakshmi rejected all the offers of Siva Tandava.

The Blessed Goddess answered:
"To give you alone joy, and to cause men sorrow,
I shall not tear my veils. With a delicate web shall
I extol mankind. I shall gather from among
All noble hearts, excellent workers.
I shall embroider new signs on my veils!
The most beautiful, the most precious,
The most powerful. And in these signs,
In the images of the noblest beasts and birds,
In the outlines of flaming flowers and
Healing herbs, I shall send to the hearts
Of people my most benevolent invocations.
I will evoke from the abyss the greatest
Creative fire. And with a rampart of flame will
I safeguard the luminous strivings of the Spirit."
Thus ordained Lakshmi.

Out from the resplendent Garden in defeat
Walked Siva Tandava. Rejoice, people!
Now shall Siva Tandava, in violent wrath
Await the long destruction of time. With
Incalculable ire, at times she crushes the earth
And then hordes of people perish. But Lakshmi,
Ever in time, casts her blessed veils. And over

The ashes of those who have perished,
Again men will gather.
They will meet in solemn procession.

The righteous Lakshmi adorns her veils with
The new sacred signs. And from out the space
    She kindles a new Fire.

1909

# Part IV

# TO THE HUNTER ENTERING THE FOREST

## TO THE HUNTER ENTERING THE FOREST

    Did Roerich give it?
    Accept it.
    Did A-Lal-Ming, Shri Ishvara, give it?
    Accept it.
    I am with him.

At the hour of sunrise I shall find thee awake already,
O hunter!
Armed with thy net thou wilt enter the forest.
Thou hast prepared thyself.
Thou art laved and alert.
Thy garments hamper thee not.
Girded up are thy loins
And thy thoughts are free.
Yes, thou hast prepared thyself
And bidden farewell to the master of the house.
Thou, O hunter, hast come to love the forest
And by thy hunting wilt bring good unto thy clan.
Thou art ready to blow thy horn.
Thou hast marked down for thyself a noble quarry
And hast not feared the weight thereof.
Blessings! Blessings! O thou who hast entered!
Are thy nets strong?
Hast thou strengthened them with prolonged labor?
Hast thou tried them with testing blows?
Art thou gleesome?
And should thy laughter scare part of the quarry,
    fear not.
But clash not thy weapons
Nor call loudly on the huntsmen.
Ah! Shouldst thou be unskillful,

From a hunter thou shalt be made a beater
And even the huntsman will be thy master.

Gather knowledge.
Watch thy trail.
Why dost thou look around thee?
Under the red stone lies the red serpent
And the green moss hides the green viper.
But its sting is all-fatal.
From thy childhood thou hast been told of serpents
    and scorpions—
A whole teaching of fear!
Many of the chirping and hissing will fly after thee
And a rustle will creep by thy path
And howling will pierce thine ear.
Worms grow into whales
And the mole becomes the tiger.
But thou knowest the essence, O hunter!
All this is not thine.
Thine is the quarry!
Hasten! Delay not, O thou who hast entered!
Waste not thy nets on the jackal.
The quarry is known to the hunter.
It seems to thee that thou wast wise yesterday
Yet thou knowest not who laid the circles of stones
On the outskirts of forests.
What do they mean?
And for whom is the sign of warning on the towering
    pine?
Thou dost not even know who filled with skulls the
    ravine
Into which thou didst cast thy glance.
But even shouldst thou be in danger,
Go not down into the ravine nor hide behind a tree.
Thy ways are without number and the foe has but one.

From the pursued become thou the attacker.
How strong are the attackers
And how weak the defenders of self!
Defense of self leave to others.
Do thou attack.
For thou knowest wherefore thou hast come forth
And why thou hast not feared the forest.

O sacred and terrible and blessed forest,
Let the hunter pass through thee!
Hold him not back.
Hide not the ways and the trail.
And terrify him not.
For I know that thou art many-voiced
But I have heard thy voices
And my hunter will take his quarry.
And thou, O hunter, know thine own quarry.

Believe not those who call thee
Nor turn unto those who would counsel.
Thou, only thou, knowest thy quarry
And wilt not choose a small quarry.
And wilt not be detained by the shadows.
Who doubts is already the enemy's prey.
Who gives way to musing loses his nets.
And he who has lost them turns backward dismayed.

But thou, O hunter, go forward!
All that is left behind is not for thee
And thou knowest this as well as do I.
For thou knowest all
And canst remember all things.
Thou knowest of wisdom,
Thou hast heard of courage,
Thou knowest of finding,

And through the ravine thou passest to mount to
   the hill.
And the flowers of the ravine are not thy flowers
And not for thee is the brook in the hollow.
Sparkling waterfalls wilt thou find
And springs shall refresh thee
And before thee shall blossom the heather of happi-
   ness.
But it blosoms only on heights
And the best hunting will not be at the foot of the hill
But thy quarry will flee over the crest.
And flaming in the skies, rising over the summit
It will come to a stand
And will look around it.
Then do thou not delay:
This hour is thine.
Thou and thy quarry will be on the heights
And neither thou nor the quarry will desire to go
   down to the hollow.

This is thine hour.
But when throwing thy net thou knowest
That thou art not a victor—
Thou hast taken only thine own.
Nor thyself count a victor
For all are victors, though they remember it not.
I have brought thee to the broad rivers
And to the boundless lakes
And I have shown thee the ocean.
He who has seen the infinite will not be lost in the
   finite,
For there is no infinite forest
And one may go round any morass, O hunter!
Together we have woven thy nets,
Together we have sought the huntsmen,

Together we have chosen the places best for hunting,
Together we have avoided danger,
Together we have made sure our way.
Without Me thou wouldst not have known the ocean;
Without thee I should not know the joy of thy winning hunt.
I love thee, my hunter!
And I shall give thy quarry to the Sons of Light.
And even shouldst thou err—
Shouldst thou for a time descend into the hollow,
Shouldst thou even look back upon the skulls,
Shouldst thou by laughter drive away a part of the quarry—
Yet I know that thou goest unweariably for the hunt,
That thou art not discouraged and wilt not lose thy way.
Thou knowest how to find thy trail by the sun
And how to turn to the road guided by whirlwinds.
But who set it afire—the sun?
And who drove it here—the whirlwind?
But I speak to thee out of the sphere of the sun—
I, thy Friend, thy Teacher, Companion on thy way.

Let the huntsmen and the leaders of the beaters be friends
And after the chase, resting on the hill,
Call unto thee the huntsmen and leaders of the beaters.
Tell them how thou didst go unto the hill
And why the hunter must not lurk in ravines,
And how on the crest thou didst meet thy quarry
And how thou knowest that this quarry is thine.
And how one must leave aside all smaller prey
For he who trails it, with it will remain.
Tell them also how the hunter bears on him all the

signs of the hunting
And how he alone knows his art and his quarry.
Tell not of the hunting to those who know not the quarry.
In the hour of trouble, in the hour of darkness,
They will engage themselves as beaters
And in the reeds take part in the hunting.
But, O hunter, recognize the huntsmen;
Drink water with them by the fire of rest.
Discern, O insightful one!
And having finished thy hunting
Mend thy nets and plan a new hunt.
Be not alarmed; seek not to alarm.
For shouldst thou alarm, a still greater fear will turn upon thee.
Plan simply.
For all is simple.
All is beautiful.
Beautiful is that which is planned.
All fear shalt thou conquer by thine unconquerable essence.

But shouldst thou begin to tremble, then defeated
And reduced to naught,
Neither crying aloud nor keeping silence,
Having lost consciousness of time, place and life,
Thou wilt lose the remnant of thy will.
Whither then wilt thou flee?
But should any of the exhausted leaders warn thee against the hunting,
Hear them not, O my hunter!
Demeanors of the will are these whose shield is a doubt.
What will their hunting be?
And what will they bring to their clans?

An empty net again?
Again unfulfilled desires?
Lost are they, as is lost their precious time.
The hunter exists for the hunting.
Hearken not to the hours of weariness.
In these hours thou art not the hunter.
Thou art the quarry!

The whirlwind will pass:
Do thou be silent.
And again thou shalt take thy horn
Without being late; fear not that thou wilt be late
And when overtaking, turn not backward.
All that is comprehensible is incomprehensible.
Where is the limit to miracles?

And one last enjoinment, O my hunter!
If on the first day of the hunting
Thou shouldst not come upon the quarry,
Grieve not—
To thee is already destined the quarry!
He who knows—searches.
He who wins knowledge—achieves.
He who has found—is amazed at the ease of the capture.
He who has seized—sings hymns of attainment.
    Rejoice! Rejoice! Rejoice!
    O thrice-called hunter!

15.IV.1921<br>Chicago

www.ingramcontent.com/pod-product-compliance
Lightning Source LLC
Chambersburg PA
CBHW071529080526
44588CB00011B/1609